# DEAF
# CULTURE
*Our Way*

# DEAF CULTURE
*Our Way*

Anecdotes from the Deaf Community

~ *by* ~

ROY K. HOLCOMB,

SAMUEL K. HOLCOMB,

& THOMAS K. HOLCOMB

*THIRD EDITION*

DawnSignPress
San Diego, California

Published by DawnSignPress
6130 Nancy Ridge Drive
San Diego, CA 92121
1-800-549-5350
FAX: (619) 625-2336

Edited by Kay Rolfe Drew

Illustrations by Frank Allen Paul and Valerie Nelson-Metlay.

Manufactured in the United States of America.

Library of Congress Catalog Card Number: 94-073905
ISBN: 0-915035-17-0

Third edition of original *Hazards of Deafness*
Second edition was titled *Silence is Golden, Sometimes*

10   9   8   7   6   5   4   3   2

# TABLE *Of* CONTENTS

# FOREWORD

*This is the third revision of the original* **Hazards of Deafness,** *by Roy K. Holcomb. The second version was titled* **Silence Is Golden,** *Sometimes. In this version, Sam Holcomb and Tom Holcomb have joined their father in revising and enlarging the original collection of anecdotes to include the most recent achievements in the deaf community such as TTYs, relay services, the latest signaling devices, etc. One section even contains incidents which have become "passe" because of some new devices which have become available to deaf individuals.*

*This anthology of anecdotes, most of which are humorous,
makes possible a new insight into the deaf community
and their culture, and also enhances an understanding
and empathy of how loss of hearing affects the whole man
and shapes his attitude and outlook on the world.
This also shows how the hearing majority reacts
whenever their paths cross those of deaf persons and
how their preconceived beliefs and prejudice
influence their reactions to deafness.*

*This should be required reading for those who may wish
to become more than casual acquaintances of the deaf community,
for these extremely readable stories will instill in the reader
a communion to deafness that no formal
textbooks can ever accomplish.*

**Leo M. Jacobs**

# INTRODUCTION

*The original version of this book, by Roy K. Holcomb,
and entitled* **Hazards of Deafness,** *was published in 1977.
That publication is considered to be a breakthrough
in the study of deaf culture, as it was the first to present the unique
way of life among deaf people through their eyes. A total of 662
vignettes were compiled that portrayed humorous, hazardous,
and sometimes embarrassing experiences of being deaf in a world
where sound predominates almost every aspect of life.*

*In response to popular demand, a new edition,*
**Silence Is Golden,** *Sometimes, was published in 1985
in a condensed form for easier reading. Specific categories
were developed to organize the "hazards" into groups such as
Traveling, Dining Out, Communicating and Mainstreaming.
This version proved to be even more popular,
selling out completely far before anticipated!*

*In an effort to update the book and make it available to the general public until well into the next century, Roy K. Holcomb's two sons, Sam and Tom, have joined together to publish this edition,* **Deaf Culture, *Our Way*.**

*New categories dealing with contemporary hazards have been created, focusing even more on the humorous aspects of the deaf experience. This edition also includes selected examples of classic "deaf" jokes which are practically nonexistent in published form.*

*We hope you enjoy our newest collection of deaf experiences,* **Deaf Culture, *Our Way*!**

**Roy K. Holcomb**
**Samuel K. Holcomb**
**Thomas K. Holcomb**

# CLASSIC HUMOR

*The following jokes have been passed down
through generations of deaf people and are widely known
among individuals within the American deaf community.
They are usually among the first to be shared
with newcomers to the deaf community.
While there may be as many versions
as there are tellers, the following stories are
presented in their basic forms.*

## *HONEYMOON*

A young deaf couple was driving down the road in a busy convention-filled city on their wedding night, looking for a room to celebrate their first night of matrimony. After finding the last available room in the entire town, the groom swooped the bride out of the car and carried her into the room. The groom was eager to begin their first night together, but the bride insisted on a bottle of champagne to make their wedding night complete. The groom grudgingly left and drove to an all-night store to buy a chilled bottle. When he came back to the motel, he could not remember in which room his bride was waiting, and the motel office was closed for the night. After a moment of pondering, he came up with a plan. He blared the horn of his car until the light of every room at the inn was turned on. Knowing that his wife could not hear the horn, he easily located his room—it was the only one with the lights out.

◆

## *SIGNING COP*

After picking up a hitchhiker on a lonely stretch of road, a deaf man was speeding down the highway. In a short while, a cop pulled him over. The hitchhiker was feeling bad for the deaf driver until it became apparent he was not getting a citation just because of his deafness. The deaf driver smiled and sped away as soon as the cop was out of his sight. Later, he was stopped by yet another cop. Once again, he pretended to have much difficulty understanding the cop, and he was let go without a ticket. The hitchhiker was so impressed that he wanted to give it a try. By that time, the driver was getting tired, so he decided to let the hitchhiker drive for a while. The hitchhiker thought this would be his golden opportunity to drive as fast as he wanted without getting a ticket. Sure enough, a cop pulled him over after clocking him at 100 miles per hour. The hitchhiker started to play deaf and acted as if he could not understand the officer. The cop started to sign, "So you are deaf. I have deaf parents. Please give me your driver's license." The hitchhiker was dumbfounded.

◆

## *ROLL CALL*

At many residential schools, it is customary for personal belongings to be labeled with students' names to prevent them from getting lost. Often, young students who have difficulty remembering all the letters in their names will look at the label to help with the spelling. One day, a student proudly wore a new shirt he just got for his birthday. When it was his turn to spell his name during the roll call, he looked at the label of his shirt and quickly spelled "J.C. P E N N E Y."

◆

## *HOLD THE JOB*

A deaf man who worked in a print shop had the reputation of being the best printer around. One day, he had been holding a piece of paper for several hours. Finally, a co-worker asked him what he was doing and why he was not working. He replied that his boss had told him to hold this one.

◆

4

## *DEAF TREE*

A lumberjack was busy working in the forest, chopping down trees. A responsible lumberjack, he would yell "Timber" each time a tree was felled. One day he came upon a tree that would not fall, no matter how hard he chopped or how loud he yelled. After consulting with his fellow lumberjacks, he decided to call a tree doctor. When the tree doctor examined the tree, his diagnosis was that the tree was deaf and could not hear the signal "Timber." The prescription was for the lumberjack to learn the manual alphabet. He mastered the alphabet and fingerspelled T I M B E R to the tree. Lo and behold, the tree began to fall.

◆

## *JOB HUNTING*

An unemployed deaf man read in the newspaper about several job openings with a company. He went into the main office of the company, wrote something on a piece of paper and gave it to the secretary. The secretary shook her head and sent him to the person above her. After reading the paper, that person also referred him to someone at a higher level. Finally, the deaf man was brought into the president's office. The president, after reading the paper, wrote "No, I want to keep my job." What the deaf person had written on the piece of paper was "I want your job" instead of "I want a job."

◆

## *CAN YOU READ?*

After observing a deaf person in a public place, a hearing man decided to approach him and find out if deaf people are literate. He wrote "Can you read?" and handed the note to the deaf person. Disgusted with this kind of ignorance, the deaf person wrote back, "No. Can you write?"

◆

## *RAILROAD CROSSING*

A deaf man was driving in the country and came to a railroad crossing with the gates down. After waiting for a while with no train in sight, he became impatient. He looked around and saw a small gatehouse by the tracks, got out of the car and approached the gatehouse. Inside was a man dozing off. The deaf man knocked on the door and asked for a pencil and paper. In an attempt to communicate his need, he wrote "PLEASE BUT." The gatekeeper could not figure out what the deaf man was trying to say, since he had no idea that the sign BUT resembles gates opening.

◆

## *KING KONG*

On a hot summer day, many people were frolicking at a local beach until King Kong appeared on the scene. Seeing the huge ape, people began to scream and hustle off the beach, except for one lovely young lady. Unaware of all the commotion, the woman continued to sunbathe peacefully. Having scared everyone away, King Kong approached the only remaining person on the beach and scooped her in his hands. She was frightened and began to scream. King Kong tried to tell her how beautiful she was. She indicated that she was deaf by pointing to her ears and shaking her head. King Kong was surprised to learn that she was deaf, since he knew some sign language. He began to sign, "You are so beautiful. I want to marry you." But in the process of signing "marry," King Kong smashed the girl into pieces.

◆

## *THE INVISIBLE HANDICAP*

A hearing man was fascinated with a deaf woman who was sitting in a bar. He decided to strike up a conversation with her by writing notes on a piece of paper. To his delight, she was friendly enough to write back. They wrote back and forth for some time. Another man jumped into the conversation and began to write too. All three continued their conversation by writing. After a while, the deaf woman realized she was late for a commitment and told her new friends that she needed to leave. The two men waved good-bye and continued to write, not realizing that neither one of them was deaf.

◆

## *BIRDS ON A TELEPHONE LINE*

A child asked his father why the birds on a telephone line were kind of jumpy while other birds on a different line were sitting quietly. After a moment of thinking, his father replied that that particular line was a TTY line, causing the birds to jump.

# OUR UNIQUE WAYS

## *OUR CULTURE*

*Deaf people have a unique culture, one that is based on sight rather than sound. Consequently, our way of behaving and thinking usually revolves around sight. This collection provides a glimpse of how deaf people function in a society dependent on sound.*

You go to a movie theater with a group of friends. In the middle of the movie, you need to go to the restroom. Upon your return, you cannot find your seat. You stand for a few moments and look for heads that are constantly shifting toward each other. You start heading in that direction since you know they are your friends—only deaf people would sign to each other constantly throughout the movie as they try to help each other figure out the plot of the movie.

◆

You usually walk facing traffic in order to keep everything within your eyesight.

◆

You are confused about whether or not people can hear bodily noises. You just can't figure out when the grumblings in your stomach are loud enough for people to hear and whether you are breathing loudly as well as hard.

◆

You call a friend. You let the phone ring more than ten times, since you know that it is possible for your friend to be home but not see the lights flash.

◆

When waiting in a busy doctor's office, you sit in a strategic location where you can easily lipread the caller and be as visible as possible so that you will not miss your turn.

◆

You are a dedicated parent who wants your young child to learn the English words for various objects in the house. You put all signs all over the house with the correct word for each object. One day, you forget to turn off the stove after using it. You decide to make a sign with the word "STOVE" on it and put it on the kitchen door to help you remember to turn off the stove each time you leave the kitchen. Your child sees the sign and says, "No, no, wrong, wrong, it's not a stove, it's a door."

◆

When running downstairs to put clothes in the dryer, you also grab your infant to keep her within your sight. Otherwise, the house could become a wreck during your few minutes of absence.

◆

When inserting coins in a soda machine, you put your hand on the machine to feel the coins drop before making the selection. Experience tells you that the machine won't cooperate until the coins have dropped completely.

◆

To prevent forgetting to turn off the stove fan, you automatically turn on the stove light as a reminder every time you need to use the fan.

◆

You feel the dashboard of your brand-new car to make sure it has started.

◆

In response to new parents of a deaf infant who ask you if you felt cheated by your deafness, you say no, but the oral education you received cheated you.

◆

You are getting ready to fly on a commuter plane to a small town. You realize that there is only one gate for eight different commuter planes. You don't know if the line forming at the gate is for the flight you want. You approach the line and peek at the destination on the tickets people are holding in their hands to make sure you don't get on the wrong plane.

◆

When introducing a friend, you quickly provide the person's background information, including hearing status, school background, affiliations with organizations, and names of mutual friends. As if this chunk of information is not sufficient, names of old flames are often given too!

◆

When visiting a deaf friend at his home, you go through a specific routine if there is no answer at the door. First you ring the doorbell long enough to make sure there is no possibility that your friend overlooked the lights. Then you check the door to see if it is unlocked. If it's locked, you walk around the building and take a look through the windows and in the yard. If it is unlocked, you ring the doorbell once again before entering. You flick the hallway light and continue your entry into the living room. After all these fail, you write a note. Otherwise, your friend will accuse you of not waiting long enough or trying hard enough to make sure he is not home.

◆

**17**

You change your doorbell light system to a cordless one. Now the chime will go off before the light flashes. Often hearing people would press the doorbell button just enough to hear the chime, but not long enough to activate the light system. You find yourself writing a note on the door, asking people to hold the button for several seconds.

◆

In order not to miss your bus, you must keep your eyes riveted on the street while everyone else casually walks around, reads or carries on a conversation.

◆

When someone asks you a question you don't want to answer you just smile, gesture "I can't hear," and walk out.

◆

Driving a car while carrying on a conversation in sign language can be tricky. As a passenger, you share the responsibility by keeping your eyes on the road and alerting the driver of any possible obstacles. That way, the driver feels more confident in maintaining the conversation over a longer span of time.

◆

Thanks to laws requiring the presence of an interpreter in the emergency room, it sometimes takes longer to receive service waiting for an interpreter to show up than by relying on the good old fashioned method of using paper and pencil to communicate.

◆

You get into a fight with a friend. She gets tired of fighting and locks herself in a room. You are determined to get the last word in, so you write a note and pass it under the door.

◆

You tap your friend on the shoulder to get his attention. After talking with him, you turn around to talk with another friend. You realize you forgot to ask the first friend something, so you turn around to tap once again and are surprised to find a different person who happened to step in at that moment.

◆

You are chatting with a friend as you walk down a busy sidewalk. You alert each other whenever you approach a possible obstacle such as a post or fire hydrant. Otherwise you run the risk of getting injured.

◆

You are discussing a hot topic. You begin to get emotional and sign furiously. All of a sudden, you knock your glasses off your head. The discussion comes to an abrupt halt while you look for your glasses, clean them up, and put them back on. Now the topic is not as hot anymore.

◆

You wait for your friend to call you back at a public pay phone. You keep your hand on the phone, waiting for it to ring.

◆

In order to say good-bye as you are leaving a party, you must "tap shoulders" one-by-one and you find yourself leaving an hour later than you had hoped.

◆

You go to a restaurant with a friend. The first thing you do after being seated is to remove the centerpiece so that you have an unobstructed view of your friend's hands.

◆

When picking a restaurant, you choose the one with the best lighting system. A poorly lit restaurant can make it difficult to carry on a conversation.

◆

In spite of all the advancements made in technology, you still need to have the lights on to communicate with your lover in bed.

## *BATHROOM TALES*

*Among deaf people, privacy is assumed when you are not visible to others. For example, behind closed doors, it is safe to think that you have complete privacy. What you can't see, you don't know. It is often difficult for deaf people to imagine how sounds can carry through walls or realize how far they can travel even with doors closed. For this reason, many stories have been shared about awkward experiences in bathrooms.*

∽

You are appalled to learn that practically every sound can be heard through most bathroom doors. You are uncomfortable at the thought of people knowing whether you had a full bladder or a severe case of diarrhea.

◆

You are never sure if it is appropriate to pass gas in a public restroom, especially if there are others in the room.

◆

**25**

You are amazed that there is a set of bathroom etiquette. You learn of this when your close friend, who happens to be hearing, alerts you to the fact that you make too much noise when you urinate in the public restroom. Apparently, you were aiming for the pool of water, which produces a splashing sound as opposed to a quieter, more polite stream against the urinal wall. You are even more disturbed because you thought you were minding your own business in a private stall.

◆

At a social gathering, you announce to your friends that you need to go to the BATHROOM instead of quietly leaving the room or using a line such as "I need to powder my nose."

◆

You are on a long flight. You need to go to the lavatory. You find a vacant one. You open the door and find someone there with his pants down. You don't know who is more shocked, you or the guy who forgot to lock the door.

◆

You are in a restroom at your doctor's office to fill a urine-sample cup. The nurse knocks on the door to see if anyone is in the restroom to let a different person in. You do not hear the knock and are caught in an embarrassing pose.

◆

You need to go to the bathroom in the middle of the night. You waltz into the bathroom and are surprised to see your mother-in-law sitting on the stool. You do not know who is more embarrassed, you or your mother-in-law.

◆

You are minding your own business in a bathroom stall. You feel someone knocking on the side of the stall. Then you see a hand waving under the divider. You are unsure what is going on. You hurry and finish. As you leave your stall, you receive a dirty look. You do not realize the person was trying to let you know that there was no toilet paper in her stall.

◆

You are uncertain how loud a noise passing gas can make.

◆

You, a gentleman, walk into a public restroom and lock yourself in a stall. A cleaning lady comes in the room after calling to see if anyone was in there. You come out of the stall, see her, and rush out, thinking you were in the women's restroom by mistake.

# NEW TECHNOLOGY, *New Hazards*

## UNSOUND TECHNOLOGY

*Many advancements in the area of technology are made
at the expense of deaf people. This collection demonstrates how
dependent society is on sound, putting deaf people at a disadvantage.*

You pull up to a self-service gas station. You proceed to pump gas in your car, unaware that the cashier had asked you over the loudspeaker to wait. You wonder why you get a dirty look when you approach the window.

◆

You do not hear your dryer beep at the end of the cycle. You find your clothes all wrinkled because you left them in the dryer far too long.

◆

You find it frustrating to shop at stores where there are sophisticated computerized cash registers. Many of them do not have screen displays for customers, making it difficult for you to figure out the exact cost of your purchase.

◆

You drive to a self-storage place to store your things. You find out that you must communicate through the intercom system to go through the gates. What makes it worse is having several cars behind you waiting for you to give the password.

◆

You are the first deaf person in town to have a car phone. You are also the first person in town having to pull to the side of the road each time you want to make a TTY call from your car.

◆

Your car begins to stall in the middle of the night on a freeway. You pull over to a call box on the side of the road. Finding yourself unable to use the phone, you are left stranded for a long time. Because of budget cutbacks, the highway patrol does not make routine rounds as often as it used to and responds to emergencies only when people call on the call box.

◆

You do not realize that machines have manners—and voices—nowadays. For example, when purchasing a can of Coke from a machine, it might say something like "Have a great COKE day."

◆

In order to serve customers more efficiently at a fast-food restaurant, you are given a number for your order. Instead of waiting for your turn in line, you now strain your eyes on the caller for your order.

◆

Fax machines are definitely a blessing, only if you can figure out the beeps. You have no way of knowing if the line is busy, since most fax machines do not have light signals for these beeps.

◆

You recently purchased top-of-the-line hearing aids. They are fully computerized and can be adjusted to fit your specific hearing needs. To your disappointment, people still give you a dirty look each time your aids whistle.

◆

You are proud of your new expensive watch that has all the latest features. You can program it so that it will beep at specific times. Unfortunately, you never know when it beeps.

◆

You are taping yourself doing an original poem in ASL about love and peace to enter in a nationwide contest. You do not realize the camcorder is also picking up the sounds from your television on a special program about the Holocaust.

◆

Even though you have installed an elaborate cordless doorbell light system, the pizza delivery man uses the knocker on the door. You wonder why your pizza has not been delivered.

◆

Many cars now come with option packages that include fancy stereo systems. You have no choice but to pay a fortune for it if you want a well-equipped car.

◆

You just purchased a new camcorder. You place your child in the prettiest part of your house so that you can tape your child's first walk for your parents, who live on the other side of the country. You do not realize that dogs were barking in the other room and the television was on with the sound blaring.

◆

You don't know if the computer is processing the data after you push the save button. You resort to feeling the terminal to see if the drive is running.

◆

You just bought a new fancy personal computer. The only printed instruction that comes with your computer is: "Congratulations! You have purchased the finest piece of technology in the world. Please listen to the audiotape for instructions on how to assemble and use the equipment."

◆

You are driving in the country in the middle of the night. You need to withdraw some money from an ATM machine so that you can purchase some gas. The machine does not recognize your password and refuses to return your card. This message appears on the screen: "Please use the phone on your right and call for assistance." You are now stuck in the middle of nowhere with no cash for gas.

◆

Beep, beep, beep. You don't realize that you have pushed the wrong button and that the computer is trying to alert you to the fact.

◆

You rent a videotape to watch with your hearing date. After the movie you rewind the tape as the closing credits begin. You do not realize that a popular romantic theme song was accompanying the credits. You lose a chance to be romantic with your date for that moment.

◆

You are not able to enjoy the convenience of the drive-through window at your favorite fast-food restaurant unless you have the audacity to get in the line, bypassing the speaker, and drive up to the window to give your order. Sometimes you receive someone else's food.

◆

The computer is down at your company. The last time it was down, it took two hours before it came back on. You loaf around, not realizing that the computer was repaired within five minutes and everyone is back to work except you.

## *TELEPHONE RELAY SERVICE*

*With the nationwide telephone relay service in place as a result
of the Americans with Disabilities Act, deaf people are able to make
calls anywhere in the country. As a result, deaf people face
new situations they never encountered before.*

∽

You try to explain to a hearing person how to use the relay service. Sometimes you succeed. Sometimes you find it easier just to say, "I'll call you."

◆

When placing an order over the phone, the process can become complicated because you need to give two sets of numbers, one for the relay and one for your number.

◆

After receiving many busy signals, you finally get through to an airline office, only to receive a computerized answer instructing you to push certain numbers to reach the designated department. Because the relay operator could not type all the information in time, you get disconnected and start receiving busy signals all over again.

◆

When you call a 900 sex line through the relay service, guess who gets the entertainment for free?

◆

As you travel through the country, you realize that the phone number for the relay service differs from state to state, unlike the operator number (0) for hearing people.

◆

You call a number through the relay service. The person answering the phone says, "No, I'm not interested in your service" and hangs up. He does not realize that the phone call is placed through a relay service at no cost.

◆

When you make a call through the relay service and receive an answering machine, more often than not the agent will need to type the message and then call again to leave your message. Sometimes, if the taped message is lengthy and spoken rapidly, the agent will need to call back just to be able to type the complete message for you.

◆

Computerized answering machines that require you to push numbers to get the right department or person can drive relay operators up the wall.

## *DECODERS*

*As recently as the late 1970s, deaf people were not able to enjoy
television programs to their fullest, since they were not captioned
and much guessing was required to understand the dialogue.
Today, almost all shows are captioned and the text appears
on the screen with a special decoder built in the television set.
Unfortunately, this technology is not without its faults.*

∽

Since local repair centers do not service decoders, you have to wait several weeks before your decoder gets repaired. You think that decoders are probably the most important invention since the wheel.

◆

Decoders are super-sensitive to interference, such as the wind blowing, although the picture often remains clear. You swear every time the wind blows!

◆

You are watching your favorite soap opera. The secret that you have been dying to find out all season long is about to be disclosed on this particular program. Just when the actress begins to blurt out the secret, an emergency bulletin about an upcoming hurricane comes on, blocking the captions.

◆

You buy a new tiny TV set. You realize you need a magnifying glass to read the captions.

◆

Since you grew up without decoders, you love watching TV now. You can't afford to miss television shows for any reason. You tape the following message for your TTY answering machine: "We are watching TV now. Please call later."

◆

You are watching the evening news on TV. The top story was about a murder. You start laughing when the captions get behind the actual dialogue and a picture of an ape appears when the name of the suspect is finally given.

◆

You continue to tape every program that is captioned. You have collections of tapes that you have not yet watched. You find it difficult to break this habit, because you remember when there were only ten hours of programs that were captioned each week, making it necessary to tape shows for nights without captioned programs.

◆

You feel that the local stations do a good job serving their deaf viewers by captioning their news programs. However, when a natural disaster hits your area, you are routinely left in the dark with no captioned emergency broadcasts.

◆

You see so many mispelled words on television that you can't help but wonder if Dan Quayle is now involved with captioning television programs after stepping down as the Vice President of the United States.

◆

You love watching local news shows on TV now that they are captioned. However, you continue to feel like a second-class citizen when the weather report comes on or when they go live with a special report, because these segments are rarely captioned.

◆

You visit a hearing relative with your parents. You pray that she has a new television, since all TV sets built after July 1993 are required to have built-in decoders.

◆

Picking your favorite news show depends on which station does the best job captioning the program.

∽

## *TTYS*

*It was not until 1965 that deaf people were able to use the telephone.*
*A coupler was developed to be used with old teletypewriters*
*from Western Union. This collection is about incidents associated*
*with the usage of TTYs that did not exist in the earlier days.*

The TTY is a device that allows deaf people to use the telephone system, provided both persons have the device on their phones. The device has allowed deaf people tremendous freedom and accessibility and is a wonderful invention, except for one small shortcoming! It is impossible to interrupt on a TTY, so if you have the misfortune of talking to a long-winded person, you must learn to do other things like file your nails or make a shopping list while waiting for him to finish.

◆

Your TTY is broken – and you can't use it to call a repair center.

◆

During a power outage, you find you're the only one in the neighborhood unable to use the phone, since TTYs depend on house electricity to operate.

◆

You get a new TTY and find it to be defective. You call the sales department of the TTY company and receive an answering message: "Sorry, our TTY is broken right now..."

◆

You tell your mother to send back her recently purchased TTY because you find it faster to talk with her through the relay service.

◆

You are in the hospital. You are provided with a phone and TTY but no signal lights. You are limited to making outgoing calls!

◆

You panic when the paper runs out in your TTY, knowing that you can't remember all the details of the gossip to share with your spouse.

◆

White pages now can indicate whether the number is a TTY one. Now burglars have a way of knowing whether the resident is deaf or not.

◆

When making a call on your TTY, you are used to two different light signals: long and slow flashes for a ring signal; short and rapid flashes for a busy signal. Nowadays, you get confused with different signals for fax, modem, voice mail and all the other features that come with phones.

◆

You receive prank calls through TTY and try to figure out who the caller is by the speed of typing, the choice of words, and the English grammar.

◆

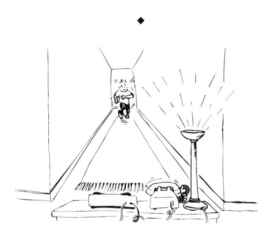

Because TTYs are expensive, you have only one. Instead of the luxury of having a phone in every room in the house, you find yourself running to the family room every time the phone rings to avoid missing calls.

◆

You have a problem with the program on your computer. You use your TTY to call the computer expert at your company. Unlike your hearing coworkers, it is not possible for you to explain the problem while keeping your eyes on the computer screen. Rather, it is necessary for you to type the message on TTY and look for your place on the computer screen and then type again on TTY and so on, making the process slow.

◆

You take your portable TTY on a trip. An emergency requires you to make a call, only to find the battery dead.

◆

At the airport, you need to make a TTY call. You find a sign indicating the location of the phone with the TTY. You follow the sign to the phone only to find a hearing person occupying the telephone booth. You are frustrated that the hearing person just happened to use that particular phone to make a voice call, even though there are many other phones around the airport.

# CLASSIC HAZARDS

*These hazards are excerpted from* **Silence Is Golden,** *Sometimes and are among the most popular ones from the original* **Hazards of Deafness**.

## *TRAVEL AND TRANSPORTATION*

Driving in a car full of hearing buddies, everyone is laughing and telling jokes. You are the driver and don't dare take your eyes off the road to "listen," so you miss out. Later, you ask your friends to repeat the jokes, but they either have forgotten them or tell them in a condensed way, and the jokes don't seem to be funny at all. This also happens when there is a hearing driver in a car full of deaf buddies.

♦

At the airport, everyone is waiting for the boarding call. Finally, they announce that people in rows 25 to 36 can board the plane. Your seat row is 7. The man at the boarding gate wonders what kind of trick you are trying to pull when you attempt to go in with the first group.

◆

On the plane, you are seated next to a blind man. Your speech is unintelligible. He keeps talking and you keep nodding, making for an unusual conversation.

◆

At a full-service gas station, the attendant asks if you want him to "fill 'er up," and you reply "yes." Then he asks if you want him to check the oil, and you reply "yes." "Water?" "Yes." Then he says something you don't quite catch, but it has something to do with tires and so you assume he wants to check the air. You reply "yes," hoping he hasn't just asked if you want four new tires or want to buy his filling station so he can retire.

◆

A pebble gets caught in your hubcap and you drive 800 clanky miles before someone brings it to your attention.

◆

Driving in your car and minding your own business, you notice people passing and pointing fingers at you. Assuming they are merely making fun of your old car, you drive on, only to find later that your tailpipe has fallen loose and is completely disintegrated because it has been dragged along the road so long.

◆

En route to California the plane runs into trouble and is rerouted to Las Vegas. After landing, the passengers are let out for a two-hour wait. Since you didn't hear the announcement, you are quite surprised to see how much California has changed with all the slot machines and casinos.

◆

Finally you arrive at your destination and check into your hotel. On the first sight-seeing tour, much to your dismay, there are tapes that have been prepared to explain interesting facts about the beautiful place you are visiting and tour guides who speak from behind a microphone, preventing you from understanding one bit.

◆

A flight attendant comes down the aisle and asks if you would like a magazine to read. You want anything except Time, but it is the only one you can pronounce clearly enough to be understood. Guess which magazine you end up reading?

◆

You start your car but don't feel the vibration because the motor is running so smoothly. You turn the key again and step on the gas, making so much noise that it sounds like a jet taking off. Passersby give you strange looks.

◆

You are driving down the interstate and the radio broadcaster announces that all cars on that road should use alternate routes to avoid a long wait. You blithely continue down the highway and end up waiting, wishing all the while that the highway department would have had the sense to put up a flashing warning sign.

◆

At a stoplight your car dies. You don't realize it until the light changes and you attempt to go. By the time you get your car started the light is red again and there is a long line of impatient drivers. You thank God you are the only one who knows you are deaf.

◆

Unbeknownst to you, your muffler has a hole in it. You drive along obliviously. Imagine your embarrassment when you get a fine for disturbing the peace.

◆

You buy a car with a built-in radio and since you have some residual hearing, as most deaf people do, you turn up the radio in order to hear it. One day a hearing friend is riding with you and you ask him if he likes the music. "What music?" he says. All he can hear is very loud static!

◆

Your car is hit by a hearing person's car. You want to call the police because you feel you are entirely innocent, but the hearing person refuses to call and leaves. There are no witnesses. You drive to the police station to report the accident but it is inconclusive who was at fault since there were no police officers or witnesses at the scene. This makes it difficult to collect from the other party's insurance company.

## *DINING OUT*

A typical meal at a coffee shop might go something like this: You are with a deaf friend, communicating by sign language. Every time you raise your fingers to sign, the waitress comes running. But when you really want something, she is nowhere to be found. She brings your order. You have ordered a ham and cheese sandwich but get a hamburger. She asks you if you want more coffee and you say no, since your cup is almost full. Later she asks what you think is the same question. You do want more and say yes. You discover as she removes your cup that the question she asked was, "Are you finished with your coffee?"

◆

One night you decide to dine in a fine restaurant, and you wait in line with others. The hostess asks if there are any parties of one who would like to be seated. When you get to the front of the line, the hostess asks how many and you reply "one." She gives you a look of annoyance, but you can't figure out why.

◆

Since you have pretty good speech, when eating out with friends you usually do the ordering and talking with the waitress. Guess who gets the check every time?

◆

You smack your lips while eating and then wonder why all at once everyone is looking in your direction.

◆

You are not able to enjoy the convenience of the drive-through window at your favorite fast-food restaurant unless you have the audacity to get in the line, bypassing the speaker, and drive up to the window to give your order. Sometimes you receive someone else's food.

◆

A man at the table next to you asks if he can borrow your sugar, but you ignore him since you didn't hear. He scowls at you as if you are very rude.

◆

In college, you were a popular guy, athletic and well-dressed. No problem with the girls. So one night on a date you decide to go somewhere really special. You take her to a high-class restaurant, acting very suave and debonair. You open the door for her and seat her at the table in a manner Sir Walter Raleigh could not have improved upon. Then when the waiter comes, your date has to do the ordering because even though you went to an exclusive oral school, you can't say "potatoes" clearly enough to be understood.

◆

One night you have a craving for a fast-food hamburger, and you rehearse exactly what to say so that they won't ask you too many questions. You tell them what you want on it, that it is "to go," and give them the exact amount of money. Then, feeling satisfied with yourself, you stand quietly and wait for your hamburger. However, the employee seems to be waiting for something else, so you repeat your order carefully. Finally she waves her arms, motioning for you to move so that she can wait on the people behind you.

◆

In a classy restaurant with a group of friends you are approached by a woman carrying a camera. She asks you several questions you can't really understand, but you assume she wants to take your picture for a fee. You have no desire to do this, so you shake your head every time she asks you something, trying hard to discourage her. After she leaves, one of the hearing people at the table is laughing his head off. He tells you that the photographer had said these things:

*Boy, do you people look sharp tonight?*
*Bet you are going to paint the town red!*
*Are you from out of town? (You are.)*
*Isn't it a beautiful evening?*
*Would you like your picture taken as a courtesy of the house?*

## *DEAF CONSUMERS*

Waiting at a pharmacy to get a prescription filled, you decide to do some shopping to pass the time. When you finish, you check back, but it isn't up on the "ready" shelf. So you do some more shopping and check back again. Still no prescription. Finally you ask what happened and find out it was put under the counter when no one answered the page on the loudspeaker.

◆

When you take things out of your pocket, many times other things come out and fall on the floor, which you don't realize until much later when you are missing something.

◆

A typical scene in a drugstore when the numbers on the cash register are not visible: The clerk says $3.30, and you interpret $3.13. He says $3.40, and you think it's $3.14, and so on.

◆

In the grocery store doing your weekly shopping you are studying the different sizes in order to get the most for your money. A woman with a cart says "Pardon me," but you don't hear and don't budge. She gets so frustrated that she slams into your cart and stomps past in a huff, when all she needed to do was tap you on the shoulder.

◆

You are doing some shopping and up ahead you notice some people moving their hands. You assume that they are deaf. Upon getting closer, you find they are not; they were gesturing to make a point.

◆

Buying a pack of gum seems like a simple enough task, but not always. You think the clerk said 90 cents, so you put 90 cents on the counter and head toward the door. Suddenly everyone is looking at you, and the clerk is having a fit. After much to-do, you realize the clerk said 96 cents, not 90 cents.

◆

Making a small purchase with a twenty-dollar bill can be unwise if you walk out without getting your change. You are halfway to China before some nice, honest person catches up with you and gives you your change.

◆

In a store it is often necessary to take a number and wait your turn. This is an awkward procedure for deaf people. You must watch the person with the number just before yours and shadow him better than Sherlock Holmes could have.

∽

## *MISUNDERSTANDINGS*

Slamming a door usually means the person is angry, but when the look on your face is a smile, this is confusing.

◆

You often drag your feet when you walk because it's a habit, not because you enjoy annoying people.

◆

Smoking a pipe is one of your habits. One day a pretty girl gives you the eye while you are smoking, and you imagine she thinks you're quite handsome and debonair. Later, a friend confides to you that you make a terrible sucking noise while smoking, and you don't feel quite as debonair.

◆

A bunch of hearing buddies and you are playing cards, and someone tells you that the noisy way you shuffle the cards drives them crazy. You end up winning the game, even though this tactic was not part of your strategy.

◆

You walk into a meeting in session, oblivious to the fact that you're making all kinds of racket and causing the speaker to lose his place.

◆

On a camping weekend you end up sleeping in your car because the campsites are all full. During the night, your leg leans against the horn, and soon everyone in the entire camp is up looking around. Some are even banging on your window. You get angry for being awakened at 3 a.m. for no reason at all.

◆

Watching television, you turn up the volume in order to hear a little, until the tenants down the hall come running in, telling you they can hear your television better than their own.

◆

One day in a supermarket, you accidentally and unknowingly knock over a display of canned vegetables. You continue on your merry way and wonder why everyone is glaring at you.

◆

Sipping your coke through a straw, especially when the glass is almost empty, can annoy a lot of people.

◆

You brush your teeth and gargle before bed each night. One night your mother comes running in and asks "What's the matter? It sounds like you're strangling!"

◆

One Sunday afternoon as you are shopping, a stranger asks you who is winning the football game. You realize he thinks your hearing aids are a radio.

## COMMUNICATING

Your brothers and sisters always liked to eavesdrop on your parents and you played along too, thinking it was great fun even though you couldn't hear a thing.

◆

Your mother is telling you and your brother and sister something very exciting, as you can see from their expressions, but you can't understand. She later tells you what it was, but not with the original enthusiasm and excitement. You wonder what the big deal was.

◆

Lipreading a person with a foreign accent is apt to make you think your eyes are out of focus.

◆

You orally tell a friend to meet you at the Acme supermarket at 10 a.m. She misunderstands you and goes to the A&P. When you see each other again she accuses you of having the world's worst speech, and you accuse her of not being able to lipread worth five cents.

◆

You start feeling sorry for yourself because no one has visited you for more than two weeks. Then you find out your flashing doorbell light has burned out.

◆

As a child you often played in the yard while your father gardened or did other chores. One day he is repairing the roof and tries to get your attention, but you are not looking in his direction. In order to draw your attention in some way, no matter how crazy, he puts on a show on the roof that would rival prime-time television.

◆

You are staying in a motel where they will serve you breakfast in your room if you call for it the night before. You aren't informed of this until morning, when you spend a long time trying to let them know that you want breakfast in your room without having to go to the front desk and tell them in person. By then you might as well have had breakfast in the coffee shop.

◆

A hearing friend tells you she is going to bowl. When someone asks for her, you tell them she went bowling. Later, someone tells you she was boating, not bowling. Finally you find out she actually went to vote.

◆

You happen to be with a hearing person and are talking, carrying on a conversation. As he talks he looks in another direction and you look too, thinking something important is going on. You continue talking and this time he looks in another direction. Then it dawns on you that hearing people sometimes look away while talking, since they don't need to lipread and don't realize how important eye contact is to deaf people.

◆

You tell a "deaf" joke to a group of hearing people. They laugh but don't understand it. They tell you one of their jokes. You laugh but don't understand it. You tell another one. They tell another one. Kindness can be carried too far sometimes.

◆

When arguing with a deaf friend who decides to shut his eyes and stop "listening," you have to figure out how to get him to open his eyes so you can finish your argument.

◆

You and your wife, who is also deaf, are watching television together. She moves. You think she wants something. You look in her direction. You move. She thinks you want something. You both move, and you both think the other person wants something. Later, you move to get her attention. She doesn't see you. Then she moves to get your attention, and you don't see her. Then you both move at the same time and both look. You both start talking at the same time. You both stop talking. You invite your wife to talk first. She talks. Then you talk. You go back to watching television. You move. Your wife thinks you want something. . .

◆

You lost a hundred bucks at the racetrack and are trying to think of a way to tell your wife the bad news. When you come home she is in the kitchen cutting up some meat with a butcher knife. You decide that this is not the right time to tell her—she might, in a fit of anger, start signing with the knife in her hand. Later her hands are busy with knitting and you decide this is the right time, since she will have to put down her knitting in order to talk back.

◆

In a large crowd of people you have spotted a friend. You wave frantically, hoping she will see you, but she looks away the moment you wave. You realize you probably look like a fool, so you pretend to be scratching your head.

◆

You are talking orally with a deaf person who was never allowed to learn sign language. Neither of you can lipread very well, and though you both have interesting things to say, neither of you can understand a word.

◆

In a dark movie theater, you suddenly want to tell your friend something. If telepathy really worked, it would certainly come in handy here.

◆

You demonstrate your lipreading abilities to the world: A guy says Wednesday and you think he said "windy." He says Thursday and you think he said "thirsty," so you invite him to a bar for a drink.

◆

Your speech is good enough to get by when talking in person, but the telephone is another story—you can't hear well enough to understand the conversation at the other end. One day you ask a stranger to make a call for you from a phone booth. He dials the number and hands the phone back to you.

◆

Few people realize that lipreading a person with a moustache is like hearing half a conversation.

◆

A person you meet tells you that you are a very good lipreader, and you reply, "What did you say?"

◆

One day as you're walking down a street, a policeman blows his whistle at you to stop. Unaware, you continue on your way. Later you are thankful you did not get your brains blown out as has happened to other less fortunate deaf people.

◆

While you're in the bathtub the phone light flashes, and you don't see it. Later, you're in the bathroom again, and the phone light flashes again. You decide to clean your closet, and the phone light flashes. Your friends ask you later where you've been all day, and you reply that you've been at home, wishing someone would call.

◆

You are looking for some friends at a convention in a small hotel. At the desk, the clerk tells you they are in room 486. You move heaven and earth to find 486 in a three-story building and finally return to the clerk and ask her to write it on paper. Then you learn something: "4 and 6" looks like "486" on the lips.

◆

Party and group situations are prime places for miscommunications with so many people talking, often at the same time. While everyone is chatting, you find yourself struggling to keep up so you laugh with the others when they laugh, frown when they frown. Soon you grow weary of this acting and decide to be yourself. Then you begin to think of something particularly funny that happened recently and smile to yourself and let out a chuckle. Everyone looks at you as if you are crazy because they are talking about a friend's serious illness.

◆

Your friend's little girl is trying desperately to tell you something. You realize what she wanted after she wets her pants.

◆

One disadvantage to being deaf is that other people who use sign language can "eavesdrop" from afar. You discover this after spending a two-hour lunch gossiping with a friend about everyone you know. Then you look up and spot a friend in the balcony who has seen your every word.

◆

While riding on a bus, you need to ask the driver for some specific directions. He answers you while looking straight ahead. You realize the only way you're going to be able to lipread him is to get on the hood and look through the windshield.

◆

You and a friend are walking down a street engrossed in a signed conversation, so much so that you don't see the woman coming with a large sack of groceries. You collide, spilling cans and boxes everywhere.

◆

A local radio station is sponsoring a contest with a prize of $1,000. Every day someone's phone rings. If the person gets the question right, they get the prize money. One day the question pertains to Christopher Columbus. You happen to be an expert on Christopher Columbus, knowing everything from the number of times he kissed Queen Isabella's hand to the number of birds that flew over his ship while he was on his voyage to the new world. Your phone rings. You try to answer it on your TTY. No answer. No $1,000.

◆

While you are taking a shower, some friends drop by to visit and your wife lets them in without telling you. You walk from the bathroom to the bedroom, giving your guests a real burlesque show.

◆

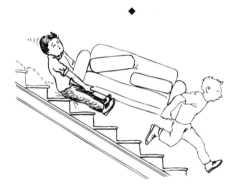

A friend has asked you to help him move some of his furniture. You are trying to move a large, heavy sofa down a flight of stairs. He takes the front and you take the rear. He is going a little too fast for you but is looking in the opposite direction, so you can't do much except hope his insurance is paid up.

## *MYTHS*

Deafness sometimes results from spinal meningitis. This is what happened in your case, and because of the meningitis, your balance is poor and your walking is uneven. One night you have the misfortune of encountering a policeman who thinks you are intoxicated and hauls you off to jail. Unable to communicate, you stay there until morning when your wife comes to pick you up. Only then do they realize you are deaf, not a drunk.

◆

Applauding as an audience member is a simple thing, unless the applause has ceased and you are the only one clapping.

◆

An accident of some sort has occurred on a busy street, and people have gathered into a large crowd. You ask a woman what happened, but you don't understand what she says. You pull out your pad and pencil and hand it to her. She walks away, thinking you are a reporter or a pest.

◆

Deaf teachers often have to deal with parents who don't want their children in their class. They assume deaf teachers cannot be good teachers because they can't speak or teach speech. Ironically, the child grows up wanting to be a teacher of the deaf.

◆

Frequently, there are rumors about a miracle cure for deafness. As a prominent figure of the deaf community, you visit schools and organizations of the deaf all around the country. Oddly enough, you have yet to encounter one of these people who has miraculously regained his or her hearing.

◆

You apply for a job where a deaf person was fired for being a slow worker. The employer assumes all deaf people are slow workers so you don't get the job, even though you have a reputation of being a fast, effective worker. You wonder how many other employers are prejudiced.

◆

When you are at a mall, you often notice people moving their hands and you assume they are deaf. You are puzzled when you discover they are not. This happens time and time again. Then you learn that hearing people use their hands when communicating, too. You remember back in school when you were told to use your hands for anything except communication, though this was what you needed them for the most.

## *MAINSTREAMING*

Many people go out of their way to avoid deaf people. They don't want to come in contact with you at all, as if being deaf were contagious. You can't help wondering if their attitude is contagious.

◆

Playing hide-and-seek as a child was always a fun game. You had to be very careful not to make noise that the hearing children could hear. You would find such a good place that no one found you and wait there for ages. Then you would discover that the game had ended long ago.

◆

Every once in a while you happen to turn around just as someone calls your name, leading them to believe that you are not deaf after all. What hearing people don't realize is that deaf people will often look around just to make sure everything is okay.

◆

Sometimes a hearing person will ask you if you know a specific word. Usually it's a simple word that even a child would know. So you play along and say "no," and let him elaborately explain it as if he were doing his scout duty for the day.

◆

You have been invited to a friend's home for a family dinner. When it's time to say grace they all bow their heads. Since you have no idea when grace is finished, you become an expert at looking out of the corner of your eye, watching for the heads to come up again.

◆

One of your "helpful" neighbors treats you as if you are helpless. She buys you groceries, volunteers to make your phone calls, scolds your children, and even gets after your husband when he misbehaves. She drops in at any time without ringing the bell until she finds you. If your lights don't come on at night, she is over to make sure everything is all right. She knows more about you than you know about yourself. But she has just one flaw – she loves to gossip. The entire neighborhood knows your every habit.

◆

A doctor thought he had the perfect solution to deafness: Stop deaf people from having children. Then someone told him that this was all well and good but that only 5 to 10 percent of deafness is inherited and that a better way to do away with deafness was to stop hearing people from having children. The doctor lost his interest in doing away with deafness.

◆

When talking with a hearing person, the conversation usually goes fine until another hearing person comes along and you are dropped cold. Then one of your deaf friends comes along, so you talk with him. Then the hearing person feels left out. . .

◆

You're at the horse races and your favorite rider is winning race after race. You get ready for the kill and put a hundred dollars on him to win. They announce a change in riders, and your horse and rider come in fourth. You wonder what happened.

◆

You have enrolled in a class and have to drive sixty miles every week to attend. You have no interpreter, but you make out by taking notes from classmates. One week, as class is breaking up, the instructor announces that there will be no class the following week. The next week you drive sixty miles and wonder what happened when no one shows up.

◆

At a meeting with an interpreter a question is directed to you. Everyone in the room has to wait until the question is relayed to you. Just hope you get the question right the first time.

◆

A well-meaning friend drags you to the opera. Once there, you find yourself watching the tails of the pianist, examining the dental work of the singers, and counting the number of people dozing off.

◆

Even when understanding nothing, you nod and act as though you do, continuing to listen to what he or she is saying. They too will nod their heads when you talk, though they too understand little. What actors we all try to be!

◆

As a youngster in a public school, recess was your favorite time of the day. One day when it was time to be dismissed, the teacher let only the girls go first. How embarrassed you were when you found yourself standing in line with them.

◆

One morning you find yourself two hours late for work because your flashing alarm clock went off when your head was under your pillow and you did not see the alarm.

◆

You remember one time in school, as the star football player, how you took the ball through the middle, throwing opponents left and right, and you ran 70 yards for a touchdown. Then you found out the whistle was blown 20 yards back where a clipping penalty occurred. Moments of glory are often short-lived.

◆

Walking past the neighbor's house, you almost get your leg bitten off by the neighbor's dog you didn't notice growling. You continue on your way, oblivious to the fact that the dog is following you, still growling. You are daydreaming about going to the National Association of the Deaf convention when all of a sudden you feel teeth in your leg.

◆

You are very surprised to find a bunch of neighbor kids in your child's room, hollering and playing cowboys and Indians. You wonder when your child let them in.

◆

One night while you're driving your car, a policeman pulls you over for running a red light, which you are sure you did not do. He comes to your window and you reach for your pad. He reaches for his gun. If you try to talk he may think you are drunk. It's very frustrating to sit while an officer writes you a ticket for something you didn't do.

◆

The television is on and across the screen flashes "Special Bulletin." You see the President's face and hope he is not announcing a nuclear war, but have to wait until the next captioned news program.

◆

Usually at the parties you attend the deaf and the hearing mingle, trying hard to communicate with one another. But by the end of the night the hearing people are on one side and the deaf are on the other.

◆

You turn on the sprinkler to water the lawn and forget about it until the neighbor calls and tells you the ocean might run dry if you don't turn your water off soon.

◆

Your block nearly burns down and every fire truck in the county is parked outside. You are inside sleeping the night away.

# A HAZARD *No More*

*Many hazards that were listed in the original*
**Hazards of Deafness** *are no longer true,*
*thanks to advancements in technology and enlightened*
*sensitivity among people in today's society.*
*The following collection is selected from the book,*
*each with an explanation why it is no longer a hazard.*

You buy a TTY. You find your phone bill a lot higher than the neighbor's because you can't type as fast as they can talk.

*In some states, TTY users receive a discount for this very reason.*

◆

You only half-close your car door and don't notice until you are on the freeway doing eighty.

*Now, with the light warning system on many cars, you are immediately alerted if the door is not closed right.*

◆

In the hospital, you can't call your loved ones, but neither can the bill collectors call you.

*Thanks to Section 504 of the Rehabilitative Act of 1973 and the Americans with Disabilities Act of 1992, hospitals are bound to provide equal access to deaf patients, including the provision of TTYs.*

◆

A news bulletin logo crosses your TV screen. Dialogue you cannot hear follows. You imagine all kinds of things happening, from Martha Raye winning a beauty contest to Martians invading New York City. You must wait until you read the next day's paper to find out what really happened.

*With an increasing number of news programs being captioned, deaf people now have equal access to information on TV.*

◆

You wait all year for Santa Claus to come, and then when he does, you can't tell when he asks if you have been good, since his beard and whiskers make lipreading impossible.

*It is now possible for you to tell Santa Claus that you have been good. Many places have special times for a signing Santa to make an appearance.*

◆

You spend half your life going to the post office to pick up captioned films or parcels that the postman wouldn't leave because he couldn't make you hear to come to the door.

*Captioned films were a popular form of entertainment before decoders were available. Deaf people would often congregate at a friend's home to watch captioned films. Trips to the post office were frequent to pick up and return films.*

◆

You are an actress who gives a super performance that brings down the house, but you fail to hear one single word of praise or applause.

*Visible applause such as handwaving is now popular.*

◆

*99*

Your tour group visits Washington, D. C. You visit many historical places – the Washington Monument, the Lincoln and Jefferson Memorials, the Capitol, and many other sites. The guides are very busy explaining about each one. Since your tax dollars built them, you just wish that you could get a little more from your tax money by being able to understand what is said.

*Interpreters are routinely provided for many tourist attractions with advance notice. You can now enjoy those national treasures as much as others.*

◆

You can't phone friends to wish them a happy birthday or invite them to a poker party. But then, neither can anyone phone you when you're in the bathroom.

*With TTYs, nationwide telephone relay service, and hearing dogs, your privacy in the bathroom is no longer assured!*

◆

**100**

You watch a football game for ages wondering what the score is before it is finally flashed on the screen.

*With the decoder, you are able to enjoy the play-by-play comments by the TV sportscaster.*

◆

You apply for a job and have to impress your prospective employer with your looks and manners rather than the spoken word. Actions speak louder than words, and it is possible to land something good if you play your cards right.

*Thanks to the Americans with Disabilities Act, deaf people cannot be discriminated against based on their inability to hear.*

◆

You arrive at the airport to go to some far-off destination. No last words can you telephone to your loved ones. You have to suffer in silence as you watch others make calls.

*Now you can suffer and battle along with your fellow travelers in trying to find an available phone.*

◆

A friend who left her address book at home is passing through your city and has no way of locating you since you have no phone and your name is not listed in the telephone directory.

*It is obvious that the deaf community has undergone a major transformation since the advent of TTYs.*

◆

You pay the full price for a TV set when you don't need the sound system. You don't mind this too much when the Miss America contest is on.

*Now that the Americans with Disabilities Act fully in place, all new television sets are sold with decoders built in.*

◆

You have a neighbor who loves to talk call your doctor for you. Soon the entire neighborhood knows your medical history, and then some.

*Privacy is now assured with the telephone relay service.*

◆

You are called to jury duty. You state that you are deaf and are easily excused. You wonder what would happen if you accepted and showed up with an interpreter.

*Deaf people are no longer automatically excused from jury duty. Interpreters are routinely provided.*

◆

You work in a factory and know every nut and bolt on every machine there. Your boss depends upon you for all the important jobs. However, when it comes time for promotions, you are quickly bypassed.

*The "glass ceiling" for deaf workers has recently been shattered, thanks to the Americans with Disabilities Act and other federal laws and regulations. The deaf can look forward to promotions and better treatment in all areas of work.*

◆

You ask a friend to make a call for you, never knowing that the message that you wanted to give and what he actually said were as different as day and night.

*Thanks to highly trained relay operators, your message is now being relayed precisely as you type it on the TTY.*

◆

You look in the classified ads for a job or a house or something, and all you find in the newspaper after each listing is telephone numbers. And Bell invented the telephone trying to help the deaf.

*Alexander Graham Bell would have been pleased to learn that deaf people are able to use his wonderful invention as well as their hearing counterparts through the use of TTYs and relay services.*

◆

Because you are deaf, all television programs, as well as movies, are "silents." You see more "silents" in a year than most people saw during the entire era of silent movies. Sad to say, most of your silents have no captions as well as no Charlie Chaplins.

*Television programs are no longer "silent," thanks to decoders. However, movie theaters are not equally accessible.*

◆

On a plane trip, you have a one-hour stopover in Chicago. You have a lot of friends there. Not one can you call on the telephone.

*Even with TTYs in the airport, you need all that time in the huge Chicago airport to make your next connection!*

◆

You spend half of your life in airports waiting for late planes since you can't phone ahead to learn if they are on schedule.

*Most airlines now have a direct TTY number. However, like your hearing counterparts, there is no guarantee that the phone will be answered by a live person instead of a computerized answering machine.*

◆

You drive fifty miles to visit a friend. You find him not at home. You leave a note under his door stating that it is very important that he see you immediately. You drive the fifty miles back home. You find a note under your door from the same friend stating that it is very important that you see him immediately.

*Your friends are now only a phone call away.*

◆

In the winter when snow is forecast, you can't listen to the school cancellations on the radio, so you wind up making the trip to school anyway.

*Many television stations provide printed information about school closures. In addition, with captioned news program, you have the same access to information as your hearing friends.*

◆

While out on errands, you lose your bankbook. To find it, you have to backtrack to all the places you have been. If you could hear, you could phone the places you had visited and would not have to go out in the cold, snowy weather.

*With the relay service, you can now pick up the phone and call those places from your cozy home.*

◆

You look out your window and see a robbery under way but have no way of reporting it until it is all over and the robbers are in the next county.

*Many police departments and 911 operators have TTYs in place, providing equal access to deaf people.*

◆

One day you have to make a phone call. You look for a person to help make your call. You find the person. You have to wait until the person is ready or is able to do so. You complete your call. On another day you have to make another call. Again, you look for a person to make your call. You find the person. You have to wait until the person is ready or is able to make it. On still another day you have to ... and such is life with the phone.

*With 24-hour relay service in place, you can make calls at your own convenience.*

◆

You and another deaf friend go to the University of Florida. You have no interpreter. Both of you take notes from a different hearing friend. After class you compare your notes and find them so different that it seems that you had been listening to two different professors.

*Interpreters are routinely provided by colleges and universities. At some places, notetakers are also assigned to deaf students.*

◆

You go to a convention on deafness. Speaker after speaker tells how deafness should be handled—and every one of the speakers has normal hearing. You wonder when there will be a convention on hearing at which every one of the speakers is deaf.

*Total exclusion of deaf people from making contributions to the field is no longer tolerated. Deaf people are now sought after for keynote presentations and active participation in professional meetings.*

◆

You are at an airport and you miss your plane because you failed to hear the last call on the P. A.

*Electronic boards near gates provide visible notices about departure times.*

◆

You take your chances in going to popular places to eat without reservations, since you don't wish to bother people to call for you. Sometimes you get in, and sometimes you are turned away and end up eating at McDonald's.

*Thanks to the relay service, reservations can be made at the restaurant of your choice–except for McDonald's, of course.*

◆

You never thrill to the phone call of a friend you haven't heard from for years or that of one who decides to call you from 3,000 miles away.

*The National Directory of TTY Numbers, known as the blue book in the deaf community, provides a list of phone numbers of at least 31,000 TTY users.*

◆

You type away and don't hear the bell at the end of the carriage, so many of your words end up beyond your right margin stop.

*Thanks to computers and automatic word wrap, there is no need to worry about the right margin endings.*

◆

You are on vacation. You leave loved ones at home and worry about them. You cannot call them, so you worry more about them. Your vacation is half-spoiled by your not being able to be reassured that all is well at home.

*Hotels are required to provide TTYs as well as decoders and flashing lights for smoke detectors and doorbell, thanks to the Americans with Disabilities Act.*

◆

During the week, you are on Cloud Nine because you can watch the ABC captioned news if you live in the right part of the country. If you can survive the weekends when there is no captioned news, you can watch the captioned news every day of every weekday.

*In some cities, every news program is captioned regardless of the day or time of the week.*

◆

You purchase a TTY and then find that in your area you can't call long distance until you first tell the operator your telephone number.

*Most long-distance telephone companies have a direct TTY number for deaf customers.*

◆

You work at a newspaper plant. At every break, workers rush to the phone to call someone. You wish you could do the same.

*Many companies now provide TTYs for their deaf workers. Instead of relaxing during your break, you now rush to the phone like your hearing peers.*

◆

**110**

You arrive at your destination and then have to find a stranger to call for someone to come and pick you up. Often the stranger you ask will misunderstand you and point to the phone where he expects you to help yourself. This is especially true when you have good speech.

*Most airports now have TTYs available for deaf travelers to use.*

◆

You buy a television set. You pay by check. The saleslady asks you for identification. She asks you for your phone number. You state that you don't have one. You purchase a car. The salesman asks for identification. He asks for your phone number. You purchase a home. The real estate people ask you for identification. They ask for your phone number. After a while, you start feeling sorry for yourself that you don't have a phone. You feel almost like getting a phone in your home in order to be able to say that you have one even if you can't hear or use it.

*You don't need to buy a phone just to say that you have one. You can use the phone as well as anyone else.*

◆

A relative dies. Because of your inability to use the phone, you are usually the last one to know.

*Many families now have a TTY in their homes, making it easy to maintain close contact with deaf relatives.*

◆

Your parents give you their phone number at work to call in case of an emergency. One day an emergency occurs. You dial the emergency number given you. You state your problem three times to be sure you get through, not knowing that the phone is busy on the other end.

*With relay service, you can be assured of clear and direct communication. No more hits or misses with emergencies.*

◆

You arrive at the airport from a trip. You can't call your wife to come and pick you up. So you shell out twenty bucks for a limousine to take you home.

*Now all you need is 25 cents to place the call from a TTY at the airport.*

# ABOUT *The Authors*

*Roy K. Holcomb* is well known for his innovative work in the field of deaf education. He spearheaded several movements including the establishment of an international organization for parents of children who are deaf, known today as the American Society for Deaf Children; the widespread acceptance of the use of sign language in schools with young deaf children through the Total Communication philosophy; and the expansion of support services available for deaf children in mainstreamed settings. In addition, Roy broke the glass ceiling for deaf administrators by becoming one of the first deaf directors/superintendents in the nation (Sterck School for the Hearing Impaired in Delaware). He is currently retired after 45 years of service to deaf education.

◆

Roy's oldest son, *Sam*, is best known for his work with ASL instruction. He has been teaching in the Center for Sign Language and Interpreting Education at the National Technical Institute for the Deaf at Rochester Institute of Technology in Rochester, New York since 1977. In 1983, he helped co-authored a series of sign language books, *Basic Sign Communication* and has since been conducting workshops nationwide on ASL instruction.

◆

*Tom*, the younger of two sons, is currently an Associate Professor at Ohlone College in Fremont, California where he teaches courses related to Deaf Studies. Previously, he taught at San Jose State University and National Technical Institute for the Deaf. Tom has published and presented extensively on issues related to education of deaf students, deaf culture, and identity formation.

# OTHER DSP PRODUCTS

# *We hope you enjoyed this book...*

DawnSignPress is a specialty publisher for instructional sign language and educational Deaf Studies materials for both children and adults, deaf and hearing. Our portfolio of materials includes exciting books and videotapes on sign language, children's stories, deaf culture, as well as school curriculum materials. If you would like to know more about DawnSignPress products, please complete the following information and send it to us.

Name......................................................................

Address..................................................................

City........................................ State..........Zip...............

Would you like to suggest someone who might like to receive our catalog:

Name......................................................................

Address..................................................................

City........................................ State..........Zip...............

How did you learn about this book? ...........................

..............................................................................

**WE WILL BE HAPPY TO SEND YOU A CATALOG.**